THE PRESIDENCY OF

Abraham

LINCOLN

THE TRIUMPH OF FREEDOM AND UNITY

BY DON NARDO

CONTENT CONSULTANT
RODNEY DAVIS
SZOLD DISTINGUISHED SERVICE PROFESSOR EMERITUS OF HISTORY
CO-DIRECTOR, LINCOLN STUDIES CENTER
KNOX COLLEGE

COMPASS POINT BOOKS
a capstone imprint

Compass Point Books are published by Capstone,
1710 Roe Crest Drive, North Mankato, Minnesota 56003
www.capstonepub.com

Editorial Credits
Melissa York, editor; Becky Daum, designer; Maggie Villaume, production
specialist; Catherine Neitge and Ashlee Suker, consulting editor and designer

Image Credits
Alamy: North Wind Picture Archives, 9, 17, 58 (top); Getty Images: Bettmann,
15, 43, Library of Congress, 50, 59 (bottom); Library of Congress, cover, 5, 6,
10, 12, 19, 20, 22, 23, 24, 27, 28, 31, 32, 34, 37, 40, 44, 47, 48, 52, 53, 57
(top), 58 (bottom), 59; National Archives, 57 (bottom); Shutterstock Images:
Adam Parent, 55
Art Elements: Shutterstock Images

Library of Congress Cataloging-in-Publication Data
Nardo, Don, 1947–
  The presidency of Abraham Lincoln : the triumph of freedom and unity / by
Don Nardo.
       pages cm.—(Greatest U.S. presidents)
  Includes bibliographical references and index.
  ISBN 978-0-7565-4926-8 (library binding)
  ISBN 978-0-7565-4934-3 (paperback)
  ISBN 978-0-7565-4942-8 (ebook PDF)
1. Lincoln, Abraham, 1809–1865—Juvenile literature. 2. Presidents—
United States—Biography—Juvenile literature. 3. United States—Politics and
government—1861–1865—Juvenile literature. I. Title.
  E457.905.N34 2015
  973.7092—dc23   [B]   2014007087

TABLE OF CONTENTS

Chapter One

Running for
PRESIDENT

A tall, lanky man with strong, bony facial features entered

a small lecture hall at Cooper Union, a New York City private

college, on February 27, 1860. His name was Abraham

Lincoln. Well-dressed in a long jacket and black tie, he did

not yet sport the beard that would later become one of his

physical trademarks.

At the time Lincoln, a Republican lawyer and former Illinois

congressman, was unofficially campaigning for president.

The national election was still about eight months away. But

Abraham Lincoln credited a photo taken the day of his
Cooper Union speech for helping him become president.
The photographer, Mathew Brady, is famous for his Civil War images.

he did not want to waste any time getting the influential men

in the Republican Party on his side. A large number of those

Republican power brokers were in the audience that evening.

Lincoln realized how important it was to make as good an

impression as possible.

The subject of the speech was slavery. More specifically,

Lincoln dealt with the question of whether slavery should be

allowed to expand. It had long existed in the southern U.S.

A political button from the 1860 presidential campaign showing Lincoln (left) on the front and vice presidential candidate Hannibal Hamlin on the back

states. And many southerners wanted to see the institution spread into recently formed U.S. territories in the West.

Like many other northerners, Lincoln was against such expansion. "Wrong as we think slavery is," he said to the Cooper Union spectators, "we can yet afford to let it alone where it is," that is, in the South. He continued: "But can we, while our votes will prevent it, allow it to spread into the National Territories, and to overrun us here in these Free [northern] States? If our sense of duty forbids this, then let us stand by our duty, fearlessly and effectively."

At first Lincoln's delivery was fairly quiet and straightforward. But as he continued speaking, his tone became more and more emotional and intense, and his listeners became increasingly spellbound. "His face lighted as with an inward fire," a reporter later wrote. "The whole man was transfigured. I forgot his clothes, his personal appearance, and his individual peculiarities. Presently, forgetting myself, I was on my feet with the rest ... cheering this wonderful man ... When he reached his climax, the thunders of applause were terrific."

The speech gave many of its listeners their first glimpse of the charisma and political genius of the man who would become one of the greatest American presidents. The Cooper Union speech was one of the most important speeches of Lincoln's career, just as he had sensed it would be. That night and in the months that followed, he won over most of the party leaders. During that period he continued to address the same issue he had tackled in the Cooper Union speech—slavery. Many other politicians of the time were speaking on the topic as well. Slavery was by far the most controversial issue then gripping American society. The country was on the verge of a civil war over whether slavery should be allowed to expand.

Some southerners had hinted they might wish to secede from the Union if Lincoln won the election.

Yet the hostility between the South and North was nothing new. While slavery was the most hotly debated issue of the day, various other regional and cultural differences had existed for decades. By the late 1850s, northerners and southerners had come to dwell in what were in many ways two distinct societies. Since the early 1800s, the North had become more urbanized, and a quarter of all northerners lived in cities by 1860. The North had also become highly industrialized, with numerous factories. In contrast, about 90 percent of southerners lived in rural areas and made their living by farming.

But the chief cultural wedge driving them apart remained slavery. A majority of southerners had either no slaves or very few, and only about one in four white families owned slaves at all. But the cotton industry was deeply dependent on the cheap labor of the South's 4 million black slaves. And the region's economy rested in large degree on the cotton industry. Many southerners, slaveholders or not, feared that freeing the slaves would bring economic devastation in the South.

To a majority of southerners, therefore, the right to own slaves seemed like something worth fighting over. Moreover, they had heard that a presidential candidate named Abraham

Lincoln believed slavery was morally wrong. Two years earlier

Senator Stephen A. Douglas of Illinois had spoken against

Lincoln. The two had debated slavery when Lincoln had

challenged Douglas for his seat in the Senate. During the 1858

Senate campaign, Douglas said that Lincoln "thinks that the

Negro is his brother." But he proclaimed, "I do not think the

Negro is any kin of mine at all." He added that the United States

had been created "by white men, for the benefit of white men."

Many southerners assumed that Lincoln wanted to abolish

slavery. At the time that assumption was incorrect. It was true

In the mid-1800s, political speeches such as the Lincoln-Douglas debates drew huge crowds.

The southern economy in 1860 was supported by slavery's cheap labor system.

that he was morally opposed to the idea of slavery. But he was not yet an abolitionist. Before he was elected president, Lincoln was concerned less with slavery's existence in the South and more with its spread into the U.S. territories. Nevertheless, growing numbers of southerners distrusted and even feared him. They were convinced that, once in the White House, he would somehow abolish slavery. On the eve of the 1860 presidential election, a Georgia newspaper editorial reflected the feelings of many southerners at that moment. Whether Washington, D.C., is "crimsoned in human gore," it stated, or "paved ten fathoms deep with mangled bodies," the South "will never submit to such humiliation and degradation as the inauguration of Abraham Lincoln."

A number of southern politicians threatened that their states would secede from the Union if Lincoln won. On election day Lincoln received no electoral votes from the southern states. He did get 59 percent of the country's total electoral votes, however, and he won the election.

Lincoln himself saw how high tensions had become. And he hoped to quiet them as much as he was able. His main objectives at the moment were to keep the Union intact and avoid civil strife. He had no way of knowing that it was already too late for both.

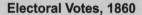

IT'S A FACT

Electoral Votes, 1860

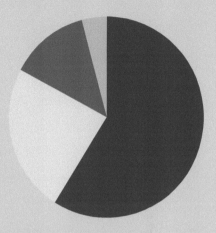

Abraham Lincoln (Republican)—180

John C. Breckinridge (Southern Democrat)—72

John Bell (Constitutional Union)—39

Stephen A. Douglas (Northern Democrat)—12

There were 303 electoral votes in the 1860 presidential election, and a candidate needed 152 to win.

LINCOLN'S LIFE

Abraham Lincoln was born February 12, 1809, in a log cabin in Kentucky's Hardin County. His father, Thomas, was a successful farmer. But when Abraham was almost 7, the family lost their land and moved to Indiana. And two years later, in 1818, Abe's mother, Nancy Lincoln, died after drinking contaminated milk. The family moved to Illinois in 1830.

When Abraham was 22, he settled on his own in New Salem, Illinois. There he found a job as a store clerk and studied in his spare time. He was almost entirely self-educated. Lincoln was elected to the Illinois General Assembly in 1834 as a member of the Whig Party. He earned his license to practice law two years later.

In 1839 Lincoln met Mary Todd, a young woman from a wealthy family in Lexington, Kentucky. They were married in 1842. Robert Todd Lincoln was born the following year. Their second son, Edward Baker Lincoln, arrived in 1846, the same year Lincoln was elected to the U.S. House of Representatives. Edward died in 1850, perhaps of tuberculosis, and the third Lincoln son, William Wallace, called Willie, was born. The Lincolns' fourth and last son, Thomas "Tad" Lincoln, was born in 1853.

In the mid-1850s Abraham Lincoln helped organize the new Republican Party in Illinois. In 1858 he ran for the U.S. Senate, opposing sitting Democratic Senator Stephen A. Douglas. The two had seven spirited debates, which history would come to decide Lincoln won. But it was Douglas who was re-elected to represent Illinois in Washington, D.C.

Undaunted, Lincoln ran for president in 1860 and won. Soon after he delivered his first inaugural speech in March 1861, the Civil War began. He became determined to save the Union and poured tremendous time and energy into managing the war effort against the Confederacy. At the same time, he faced another personal tragedy—Willie Lincoln died in February 1862.

In large part thanks to Lincoln, the war increasingly went in the North's favor. He was re-elected president in November 1864 but would not serve out his second term. Discontented actor John Wilkes Booth shot Lincoln on April 14, 1865, in Ford's Theatre, in the U.S. capital. The president never regained consciousness, and his life ended the next morning. He was succeeded by his vice president, Andrew Johnson.

Chapter Two

Saving
THE UNION

In the wake of Abraham Lincoln's victory in the 1860
presidential election, dire predictions flooded the South.
Many people were sure that the new president would soon
free all the slaves. They feared ending slavery would lead to a
race war in which enraged African-Americans would disrupt
society. "In TEN years or less," a white Georgian warned, "our
CHILDREN will be the *slaves* of negroes." Others claimed that
with the sudden loss of slave labor, the South's economy would
be destroyed.

Lincoln's election prompted contentious meetings about secession throughout the South.

There was only one way to avoid these or even worse calamities, many southern leaders claimed. Namely, the southern states must secede from the Union and establish their own nation. This sentiment spread among the men making up South Carolina's legislature. And on December 20, 1860, every one of them voted to separate from the United States. They both hoped and expected other southern legislatures would follow their lead in the weeks and months ahead.

President-elect Lincoln also expressed hope. He hoped

that he could find a way to keep other states from following

South Carolina's lead. He sent a letter to Georgia Congressman

Alexander Stephens on December 22. Lincoln asked, "Do the

people of the South really entertain fears that a Republican

administration would, *directly, or indirectly,* interfere with their

slaves, or with them, about their slaves?" If so, he went on,

"there is no cause for such fears."

Yet those fears were real and did not subside. Five more

southern states—Mississippi, Florida, Alabama, Georgia, and

Louisiana—left the Union by February 1, 1861. Three days

later representatives from the seceded states assembled in

Montgomery, Alabama. There they founded a new country,

the Confederate States of America. It came to be called the

Confederacy for short. Texas seceded in March.

Lincoln was disturbed by this turn of events. He believed

it was his duty as president to prevent states from seceding,

at any cost. Hoping to convince the rest of the southern states

to stay in the Union, he said in public what he had written

Alexander Stephens privately. In his first inaugural address, the

new president spoke of an "apprehension" that "seems to exist

among the people of the Southern States." They think that "their

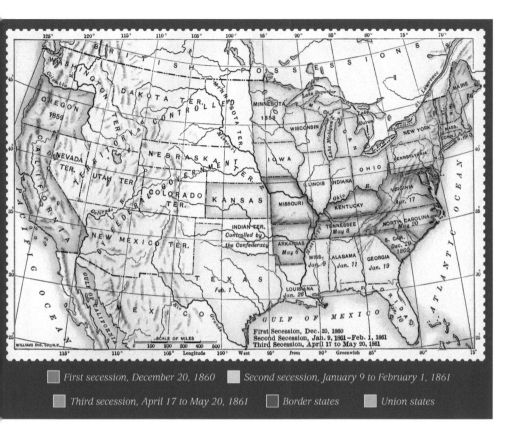

First secession, December 20, 1860   Second secession, January 9 to February 1, 1861

Third secession, April 17 to May 20, 1861   Border states   Union states

property, and their peace, and personal security" somehow

"are to be endangered." Yet, he said, "There has never been

any reasonable cause for such apprehension. Indeed, the

most ample evidence to the contrary has all the while existed,

and been open to their inspection. It is found in nearly all the

published speeches of him who now addresses you."

This assurance was not enough for the remaining southern

states, however. In April and May 1861, North Carolina,

Virginia, and Arkansas seceded and joined the Confederacy.

The northwestern part of Virginia broke away and became the

northern state of West Virginia, siding with the Union. In May 1861 Tennessee would become the last state to secede. Some border states on the edge of the Confederacy that allowed slavery stayed with the Union—Delaware, Kentucky, Maryland, and Missouri.

Lincoln found himself in a delicate and potentially dangerous position. A U.S. military base—Fort Sumter—lay on a small island in the harbor of Charleston, South Carolina. The Confederates believed that it and other bases on their lands belonged to them. But Lincoln disagreed. To demonstrate that the fort still belonged to the U.S., he sent ships to resupply it. In response, the Confederates attacked the fort on April 12, 1861, thereby igniting the American Civil War.

Three days after the attack on Fort Sumter, Lincoln called for 75,000 volunteers to put down what he referred to as an insurrection. There was never any question in his mind that the southern states' secessions were illegal. Therefore, he reasoned, those states must be brought back into the Union. And if force was necessary, so be it. He firmly believed it was his duty as president to preserve the nation the founding fathers had created in the 1770s. Northerners agreed with him with very few exceptions and spoke out against the division of

Union forces surrendered Fort Sumter after a 34-hour Confederate bombardment; there were no battle casualties.

the Union. An Ohio official wrote that Lincoln "must enforce the laws of the U. States against all rebellion, no matter what the consequences."

At first Lincoln hoped that bringing the Confederate states back into the fold would take only a few months. The initial northern plan was to use the volunteer army to defeat the southern rebels. Then they would arrest the president, Jefferson Davis, and his advisers. After that, it was hoped, the other southern leaders would give up and the insurrection would end.

But this proved to be wishful thinking. Southern forces won the war's opening battle, today called First Bull Run or First Manassas, in eastern Virginia. The Confederacy then raised more armies and put up a stiff and at times courageous fight.

Over time, however, it became clear that the southern states had no credible chance of decisively defeating the North. The Union simply had too many large-scale advantages. Its population was much bigger than the South's. And its industries and factories were superior.

Still another major northern asset that the South could not match was a commander in chief of extraordinary talent and vision. Lincoln had had little formal military training before the war. Yet he possessed a wealth of inborn instincts and talents

After the first battle of Bull Run, both sides thought the conflict would be over quickly. It would take time for the North's advantages in supplies and manpower to tell.

that made him an outstanding natural leader. He was shrewd, a good judge of character, and an amazingly quick learner. He also had a superb sense of timing.

In fact, the consensus of modern historians is that Lincoln was more talented in military affairs than the officers he commanded. Military historian T. Harry Williams called him "a great natural strategist, a better one than any of his generals. He was in actuality as well as in title the commander in chief." Williams added that Lincoln "did more than" any of his generals "to win the war for the Union."

These innate abilities often allowed Lincoln to grasp the right strategy for the time and place. He realized early on that the North's greater numbers could be used to put constant pressure on Confederate lines. Then, when a weak spot was found, one or more northern armies could make a breakthrough. Lincoln also recognized that the North's sea power could help isolate the Confederacy. Northern ships strove to control all of the nation's seacoasts and the Mississippi River. This made it increasingly difficult for southern states to import badly needed arms and other supplies. Furthermore, Lincoln sensed when it was more effective to target enemy armies and when it was time to attack Confederate cities.

The political effects of the war were never far from Lincoln's mind. He appointed many high-ranking officers in the army not for their military know-how but for their political connections or ties to ethnic groups. What he sacrificed in battle experience he gained back many times over in securing the loyalty and aid of the large groups of people that his political appointees mobilized for the war effort.

At the time few Americans realized Lincoln's innate talents as a military and political strategist. In fact, he was often criticized for being incompetent as a military leader. Practically every time the North lost a major battle, particularly in the

Lincoln (left) met with General George McClellan at Antietam on October 3, 1862, two weeks after the battle. The Battle of Antietam was the bloodiest single day in U.S. history.

OF, BY, AND FOR THE PEOPLE

A few months after the battle of Gettysburg (July 1–3, 1863), President Lincoln traveled to the site of the encounter in Pennsylvania. In a short but moving speech to dedicate a national cemetery, he paid tribute to the thousands of soldiers who had fought there. He confirmed the words of the nation's founders, that "all men are created equal." Those who had died had given their lives for a noble cause, he said. He explained that the Civil War was a test of whether the nation's values and unity could endure. "We have come," he stated, "to dedicate a portion" of the battlefield "as a final resting place for those who here gave their lives that [our] nation might live." His tone growing more dramatic, he continued, "From these honored dead we take increased devotion to that cause for which they gave the last full measure of devotion ... We here highly resolve that these dead shall not have died in vain—that this nation, under God, shall have a new birth of freedom, and that government of the people, by the people, for the people, shall not perish from the earth."

Lincoln gave the Gettysburg Address November 19, 1863.

war's early years, many northern officials and newspaper editorials blamed him. In one major battle after another, the South suffered thousands of dead and wounded. Northern battle casualties were also high. But the strategic military approaches Lincoln advocated caused the Confederacy to grow war-weary considerably faster than the Union did. And the Union had a far larger pool of men to draw on to replenish its military ranks.

The Confederacy's fortunes continued to wane. The South's capital at Richmond, Virginia, fell to Union forces April 3, 1865.

Lincoln was criticized in the press for the war's many casualties.

And only three days later, the Confederates endured a terrible defeat at Sayler's Creek, southwest of Petersburg, Virginia. Sadly and soberly, Confederate General Robert E. Lee concluded that further bloodshed was futile. He formally surrendered to Union General Ulysses S. Grant on April 9.

News of the surrender soon reached Washington, D.C. Lincoln felt as if a heavy weight had been lifted from his shoulders. His primary goal—saving the Union—had been accomplished. Not long afterward, in his second inaugural address, he called on Americans on both sides to put their differences behind them. That way they could march together into a brighter future for all. This should happen, he said, "with malice toward none" and "with charity for all."

Chapter Three

Freeing
THE SLAVES

When he was a child, Abraham Lincoln attended a Baptist church where most members opposed slavery. So the idea that it was wrong for one person to own another was ingrained in him from an early age. Yet for a long time, he did not foresee that anything could be done to stop the immoral custom. He assumed that slavery was simply an inevitable fact of life.

Lincoln's views on slavery and the position of African-Americans in the United States changed, although very slowly, beginning when he was an Illinois legislator in the 1840s.

Lincoln's views on slavery and race changed throughout his life.

As that decade started, he viewed slavery and the equality of black people as two different things. He initially felt that African-Americans were not socially equal to whites. This explains why he supported an 1829 state law that banned marriage between whites and blacks.

Later, in the early to mid-1850s, Lincoln held the same position on slavery that many educated, thoughtful northerners then did. He held that the institution was a bad thing. But he was not sure what could be done about it. Six years before he ran for president, in 1854, he explained in a speech: "If all earthly power were given me, I should not know what to do, as to the existing institution. My first impulse would be to free all the slaves and send them to Liberia [in Africa] ... But a moment's reflection would convince me ... its sudden execution is impossible. What then? Free them, and make them politically and socially, our equals? My own feelings will not admit of this;

Once he was in the White House, Lincoln met with African-American abolitionists and activists including Sojourner Truth.

and if mine would, we well know that those of the great mass of white people will not ... We cannot then make them equals."

Lincoln still did not support freeing all the slaves in 1858. But by then he was strongly against the expansion of slavery into the western territories. In fact, he said, this would threaten the very unity of the country. That year he addressed the issue in what later came to be seen as one of his most famous speeches. "A house divided against itself cannot stand," he said. "I believe this government cannot endure, permanently half *slave* and half *free*." In the long run, he continued, "It will become *all* one thing or *all* the other. Either the *opponents* of slavery, will arrest the further spread of it ... or its *advocates* will push it forward, till it shall become alike lawful in *all* the states."

Lincoln did not want slavery to become "lawful in *all* the states." That meant, by his own logic, that sooner or later it would be necessary to begin freeing the slaves. Yet that necessity did not become a priority for him until the Civil War had been raging for several months. Steadily he saw the wisdom of freeing various groups of slaves. He agreed when Congress freed the slaves in the nation's capital, Washington, D.C., in April 1862. And soon after, on June 19, Lincoln signed a law passed by Congress that abolished slavery in the U.S. territories.

THE RACES TO LIVE APART?

For a long time, Lincoln assumed it would be better for members of the white and black races to live apart. This was based on his belief that they lacked fundamental equality. In September 1858, for instance, he said, "I am not, nor ever have been, in favor of bringing about in any way the social and political equality of the white and black races." Nor did he favor allowing blacks "to intermarry with white people." Lincoln's initial solution, as others had proposed before, was to free black people and then resettle them somewhere outside the United States. He hoped colonization would make emancipation easier for voters to swallow in the border states. Possible locations discussed included Africa, Central America, or the Caribbean. He eventually abandoned this approach. African-American leaders including Frederick Douglass and much of the black population were against it. Growing numbers of American abolitionists were not in favor, and the political situation in the border states had stabilized. Also, economists realized blacks were and should remain an essential part of the U.S. labor force. Finally, diplomats from several of the lands proposed to receive the former slaves vigorously protested the resettlement plan.

The president had also been thinking about issuing a major proclamation that would free the slaves held in the South. As with the ban on slavery in the territories, his primary goal was not the total abolition of slavery. Instead, these moves were mainly designed to help the North defeat the South. Lincoln hoped that when southern slaves heard about such laws freeing them, they would be inspired to run away. The desired result would be a major disruption of southern society. Another reason he felt it was neither practical nor wise to ban slavery everywhere in the country was to make sure the North

remained intact. He worried that an overall ban on slavery

might prompt some northern border states, including Kentucky,

to join the Confederacy.

As Lincoln told a prominent newspaper editor August 22,

1862, "My paramount object in this struggle *is* to save the

Union, and is *not* either to save or to destroy slavery. If I could

save the Union without freeing *any* slave I would do it, and if I

could save it by freeing *all* the slaves I would do it; and if I could

Cartoons criticized Lincoln's willingness to compromise on slavery in order to save the Union.

save it by freeing some and leaving others alone I would also do that. What I do about slavery, and the colored race, I do because I believe it helps to save the Union."

Lincoln issued the order freeing slaves in areas of the South in rebellion January 1, 1863. It became known as the Emancipation Proclamation. The document stated in part that "all persons held as slaves within said designated States, and parts of States" listed in the document as in rebellion "are, and henceforward shall be free."

The Confederate states, however, did not recognize Lincoln's authority. So this executive decree freed no one.

July 22, 1862, draft of the Emancipation Proclamation

The North had to win the war to make good on Lincoln's promise. The complete eradication of slavery in the United States was accomplished by the Constitution's 13th Amendment. It was adopted in December 1865, several months after Lincoln's death.

Nevertheless, the 1863 proclamation did serve its purpose. A number of southern slaves took heart and escaped bondage. Several European nations, which strongly opposed slavery, now stepped up their support for Lincoln's government. He rightly recognized the document's importance when he signed it. "If my name ever goes into history," he declared, "it will be for this act."

Some northern abolitionists severely criticized Lincoln's efforts at freeing slaves during the war. They wanted the government to free all the slaves immediately. Lincoln realized that abolition could be successful only if it was done in stages. But the most passionate abolitionist leaders rejected his arguments and condemned him.

Despite his critics, the evolution of Lincoln's views on slavery continued. After freeing specific groups of slaves, he increasingly recognized that all the slaves would eventually need to be emancipated. One important result of his changing

*African-Americans escaping slavery found freedom
when they reached Union army camps.*

positions on the subject affected the military—a reversal of his

former policy on creating black regiments in the Union army.

At the outset of the war, he had opposed it, worried the border

states would secede. After the Emancipation Proclamation,

Lincoln approved the formation of black regiments. By the end

of the war, almost 200,000 black soldiers and sailors had fought

for the Union.

Lincoln paid tribute to black Union soldiers: "With silent tongue, and clenched teeth, and steady eye, and well-poised bayonet," he wrote, "they have helped mankind." He would never have penned such words a decade before. Like other white people, back then he could not have conceived of whites recruiting blacks to fight other whites. His statement was therefore a vivid illustration of how much his views on African-Americans and their rights and abilities had changed.

Expanding
THE NATION

Even while Abraham Lincoln wrestled with and agonized

over the course of the war and the issue of slavery, he was

also attending to many other priorities. He had begun setting

his sights beyond the end of the war to the reunited country's

future. In his mind it was vital to ensure that the nation kept

looking forward and expanding in the decades that followed.

He was thinking not only of his own presidency but of the

long-term future of the country.

The country's westward expansion continued during the Civil War.

There were certain projects the government could tackle in pursuit of that objective. One was to motivate and help American settlers to move into the lands between the Mississippi River and the Pacific Ocean. Another was to build railroad lines that would carry American settlers and their supplies westward. At the time most of the western lands were inhabited by Native Americans. But that fact was of little or no consequence to white people. They argued that the American Indians had not physically developed those lands, so they could not lay claim to owning them. Therefore the regions in question belonged to whoever *could* and *did* develop them— white settlers.

The question was whether to invest time and money in such projects while the conflict still raged. Or should the government focus on one major goal at a time and wait until the war was over to plan for the future? Lincoln was fortunate that Congress mostly agreed with the idea of launching expansion sooner rather than later.

The idea of exploiting the vast lands in the West was not new to either Congress or Lincoln. In the 1850s several members of Congress had suggested that the government grant some of these lands to American settlers. That way the region would come to have a network of farms, homes, towns, and

White settlers were eager to begin settling the Great Plains throughout the second half of the 1800s.

roads. The nation's population would increase, along with its economic prosperity and power.

Legislative bills that would grant western lands to settlers came to be called homestead acts. Several such bills had been considered by Congress during the 1850s, before Lincoln became president. But they were blocked, mostly by southern legislators. In the southerners' view, if such plans were enacted, the West would fill up with transplanted northerners who would make slavery illegal there.

Most of the opposition fell away, however, when the southern states seceded in 1860 and 1861. The members of the 37th Congress eagerly arrived in Washington, D.C. Republicans held a hefty majority in the House of Representatives and controlled the Senate.

Overall, a vocal minority of radical Republican members dominated the new Congress. In a political context *radical* usually means very socially progressive. Similar to the head of their party, President Lincoln, they had strongly opposed the South's separation from the Union. Congress gave the new chief executive nearly every military tool he needed to defeat the South, along with much more. Because of the secessions, the South no longer had any power in Congress. Although Lincoln

CAPTAIN OF THE TEAM

Lincoln possessed political wisdom and skills that outshone those of most other presidents, according to scholar Doris Kearns Goodwin. This is particularly evident, she says, in his so-called team of rivals. After winning the 1860 election, Goodwin wrote, Lincoln "made the unprecedented decision to incorporate his eminent rivals into his political family, the cabinet." In winning the Republican nomination for president he had defeated three political heavyweights—William H. Seward, Salmon P. Chase, and Edward Bates. Yet he later convinced Seward to become secretary of state, Chase secretary of the treasury, and Bates attorney general.

This unorthodox approach to governing, Goodwin said, was "a first indication of what would prove to others a most unexpected greatness." Lincoln emerged as "the undisputed captain" of a true "team of rivals." Over and over again, "he was the one who dispelled his colleagues' anxiety and sustained their spirits with his gift for storytelling and his life-affirming sense of humor." Moreover, he was very successful "in dealing with the strong egos of the men in his cabinet." In Lincoln's own time, his good friend Leonard Swett summed up this same unique political strength. Lincoln "managed his politics upon a plan entirely different from any other man the country has ever produced," Swett remarked.

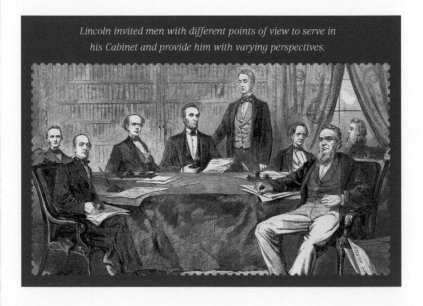

Lincoln invited men with different points of view to serve in his Cabinet and provide him with varying perspectives.

and Congress did not always agree, no other president, before or since, had so much congressional support for legislation of all sorts.

Lincoln recognized this unique opportunity and took full advantage of it. He regularly lobbied lawmakers to pass bills he felt would either save or expand the Union. Scholar James MacPherson has called that Congress "one of the most productive in American history."

One of the biggest and most far-reaching components of this avalanche of congressional legislation was the Homestead Act. It passed the House by an impressive 107 to 16 margin and the Senate by 33 to 7. Lincoln signed it into law May 20, 1862, thereby opening up enormous tracts of land to settlers. With a few qualifications, anyone who applied for and then lived on and developed a 160-acre (65-hectare) plot for five years gained ownership of it.

Spurred on by Lincoln, Congress also sought to provide the farmers and town builders with the tools and skills they required to be successful. A key

IT'S A FACT

Before the end of the war, the government received more than 25,000 applications for homesteads. By 1900 more than 500,000 farm families had used the act to settle on 80 million acres (32 million hectares) in the rapidly expanding West.

development was expanding the country's railroad network. Lincoln signed the Pacific Railway Act on July 1, 1862. It helped fund the first transcontinental line. One construction crew began in California. The other started in Omaha, then the capital of the Nebraska Territory.

The two lines of track converged at Promontory Summit, Utah, on May 10, 1869. Thereafter settlement of the West was much faster and easier than before. Before the new line, it had taken several months to travel—by either ocean or land—from the East Coast to California. With the new railroad, it took less than 10 days.

The transcontinental railroad was not the only tool that benefited the thousands of new western settlers. Lincoln signed into existence the U.S. Department of Agriculture on May 15, 1862. Its initial purpose was to help farmers develop their lands. One way was by promoting the most advanced scientific farming methods then known. From the start the agency proved itself immensely valuable to the country's land development and food production. The president proudly called it "the people's Department."

During the decades following Lincoln's presidency, new settlers also gained needed skills through the Morrill Land

*Railroad executives used a golden railroad spike to celebrate
the completion of the transcontinental railroad.*

Grant Colleges Act. Lincoln signed it into law July 2, 1862. The
act provided funds for the states to open colleges that taught
farming and industrial skills.

The Morrill Act's impact over time on American education
and society was huge. Its schools include many of today's state
universities that have educated millions and contributed greatly
to research and scientific advancement.

The homesteading, railroad, and land grant college acts all
helped make the country both bigger and stronger, examples of
Lincoln's principal goal. More than anything else, he wanted to

Lincoln's political savvy and vision for the future set the scene for many changes in the late 1800s and early 1900s.

save and strengthen the Union. Politically speaking, therefore, he was a nationalist, a patriot devoted to protecting and bettering the nation. Almost by default the bills he supported also strengthened the central, national government. This often happened at the expense of the powers of individual states.

Lincoln pushed for another bill that increased the central government's influence and power. It was the National Banking

Act of 1863. Prior to it many individual banks issued their own currencies. The new banking system Lincoln installed established a single national currency used everywhere in the country. The banking act shaped economic and social institutions and customs for generations to come.

In a very real way, James McPherson said, with Congress Lincoln created a "new America." Scholar Leonard Curry concurred, suggesting that Lincoln and Congress drafted "the blueprint for modern America." To whatever degree this is true, nearly all historians agree on one point. Part of what made Lincoln a great leader was his ability to massively remodel the nation even as he was preventing a bloody war from utterly destroying it.

Chapter Five

Belonging
TO THE AGES

In the autumn of 1864, Abraham Lincoln's first term as president was drawing to a close. By that time he had signed into law a large amount of legislation that was destined to help shape the nation's future. But the Civil War was still raging. And a worry hung heavily on him. It was possible he might be defeated in the upcoming November election.

There were good reasons for such a worry. Some Americans blamed Lincoln for what they saw as a failure to end the awful conflict sooner. Speaking for those who held this view were

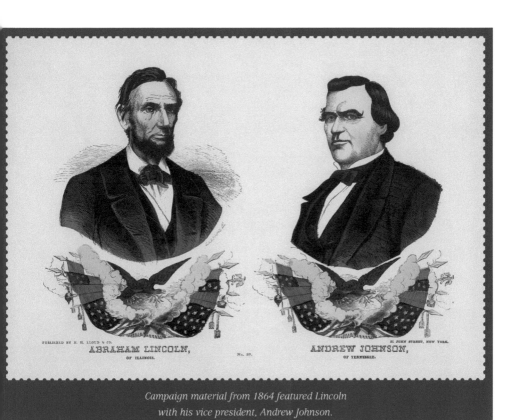

*Campaign material from 1864 featured Lincoln
with his vice president, Andrew Johnson.*

Lincoln's major political opponents in the North, the Democrats.

Leaders of the party demanded that he cease hostilities and

offer to negotiate an honorable peace with Confederate leaders.

Perhaps even more distressing to the president was that

some members of his own party were unhappy with him.

The more radical Republicans felt he was not committed

strongly enough to recognizing the equality of former slaves

after the war's end. The radicals also criticized his plans for

reconstructing the South following the conflict. They felt he

would be too forgiving to individuals and states they believed

A cartoon depicts Lincoln (left) as the antislavery candidate and McClellan as a southern sympathizer shaking hands with Confederate president Jefferson Davis (far right).

should be harshly punished. For a while it looked as though Lincoln might lose the support of an entire wing of the Republican Party.

As the election drew near, however, most of the radical Republicans did not abandon the president. His main opponent remained the Democratic nominee for president, General George B. McClellan. McClellan had been commander of Union forces early in the war. Lincoln had fired him for a lack of energy and initiative.

During the 1864 campaign, the Democrats called Lincoln a despot who had abused his presidential authority. Some of the laws and decrees he had issued while fighting the war had been unconstitutional, they claimed. The main example had been his suspension of habeas corpus in late April 1861. Habeas corpus is the legal concept that a person cannot be kept in jail without a fair hearing in court. The government must show a good reason to continue holding him or her. Lincoln temporarily suspended this rule so that the Union could keep suspected southern sympathizers in prison. He feared that they might interfere with federal troops who were trying to put down the South's rebellion.

The following month Roger Taney, then the Supreme Court's chief justice, pointed out that the Constitution gives only Congress the power to suspend habeas corpus. Therefore, Lincoln lacked the authority to do that. Lincoln ignored Taney and kept the suspension intact for a while. The president finally restored habeas corpus in February 1862, but by that time the damage to his reputation among his critics had been done.

During the 1864 presidential campaign, however, a majority of Americans disagreed with those criticisms. The election was not nearly as close as many people, including Lincoln himself, had expected. The fall of Atlanta, Georgia, on September 2 helped seal Lincoln's win. The president won a commanding

At his second inauguration on March 4, 1865, Lincoln (circled) spoke about the war's end. He sought "to bind up the nation's wounds" to create "a just, and a lasting peace."

victory, receiving 212 electoral votes. McClellan got only 21. The president also won a respectable 55 percent of the popular vote.

Lincoln's win would have allowed him to remain president at least until 1868. He might even have won the subsequent elections in 1872 and 1876. At that time there was not yet a limit of two terms set on the presidency. But none of those scenarios would come to pass. Accompanied by his wife, Mary Todd Lincoln, and others on April 14, 1865, Lincoln attended a play at Ford's Theatre in the U.S. capital.

Presidential aides had warned the president not to mingle in public crowds. He had recently given a speech in which he had advocated granting voting rights to some former slaves. The aides feared that this might incite racists—northern as well as southern—to try to kill him. But Lincoln decided to go to the play anyway. His attitude was that there was no realistic way to stop a committed assassin. Earlier he had told an associate, "I long ago made up my mind that if anybody wants to kill me, he will do it."

Unfortunately for Lincoln and the nation, just such an assassin appeared. John Wilkes Booth was a well-known actor and a southern sympathizer. He viewed blacks as inferior to whites and hated Lincoln. The president's recent speech about black voting rights had indeed convinced him that Lincoln must die. So during the performance at Ford's Theatre, Booth slipped into the box where the Lincolns were sitting. There he shot the president in the back of the head.

Booth managed to escape the theater. But he was killed 10 days later as soldiers moved

IT'S A FACT

John Wilkes Booth's assassination of Lincoln was part of a wider plot. A band of conspirators sought to slay the secretary of state, William H. Seward, and other major government officials. Lincoln was the only fatality.

in to capture him. The president did not die immediately. After the shooting he was carried to a nearby boardinghouse. There members of his family and presidential Cabinet crowded around his bedside. Doctors held no realistic hope for his recovery. And at 7:22 the next morning, April 15, 1865, Abraham Lincoln died. The silence in the room was broken by Secretary of War Edwin M. Stanton. His voice wavering in his grief, he said softly, "Now he belongs to the ages."

Ford's Theatre box where Lincoln was shot

Lincoln is remembered as the emancipator and the preserver of the Union.

The words spoken at Lincoln's deathbed convey a profound truth. The 16th president was loved by some but despised by many others during his lifetime. Yet after his passing, his reputation grew, at times with startling speed. By the first half of the 20th century, a majority of Americans looked back on him as the nation's savior.

Today leading presidential historians consistently rate him either first or second among the greatest presidents. The main reason cited by the scholars is that Lincoln successfully guided the country through two immense crises. The Civil War had torn

A MODEL FOR ALL GENERATIONS

Michael Burlingame, who ranks among Lincoln's leading modern biographers, has described many of the qualities that made the 16th president an inspiration to people everywhere. One of these, Burlingame points out, was an ability to succeed against what many might see as impossible odds.

"Few will achieve his world historical importance," said Burlingame, "but many can profit from his personal example, encouraged by the knowledge that, despite a childhood of ... grinding poverty, despite a lack of formal education, despite a series of career failures, despite a miserable marriage, despite a tendency to depression ... he became a model of psychological maturity, moral clarity, and unimpeachable integrity. His presence and his leadership inspired his contemporaries. His life story can do the same for generations to come."

the nation asunder, and he did more than patch it back together. He also had a major hand in the process that abolished the inhumane institution of slavery in the United States.

Historians regularly list other factors that made Lincoln a great president. He signed the Homestead Act and Pacific Railway Act into law. These and other major pieces of legislation laid the groundwork necessary for the country to expand from ocean to ocean in the decades following his death. His skill at managing the competing political factions around him is generally regarded as genius.

For these and other reasons, historians and political leaders in each generation have come to recognize Lincoln's

IN THIS TEMPLE
AS IN THE HEARTS OF THE PEOPLE
FOR WHOM HE SAVED THE UNION
THE MEMORY OF ABRAHAM LINCOLN
IS ENSHRINED FOREVER

The Lincoln Memorial in Washington, D.C., honors the 16th president.

almost unmatched talents and accomplishments. One such

voice from his own generation belonged to Union general

and future president Ulysses S. Grant. He called the president

"incontestably the greatest man I ever knew."

The generations that followed held Lincoln in such esteem

that they created memorials of all kinds for him. They placed his image on two forms of U.S. currency, the penny and the $5 bill. They also erected the magnificent Lincoln Memorial in Washington, D.C., and carved his face on Mount Rushmore in South Dakota.

As Barack Obama, the first African-American U.S. president, explained, "Lincoln saw beyond the bloodshed and division" of the Civil War. "He saw us not only as we were, but as we might be. And he calls on us through the ages to commit ourselves to the unfinished work he so nobly advanced—the work of perfecting our Union."

Historian James McPherson agreed. "More than any other American," he wrote, "Lincoln's name has gone into history. He gave all Americans, indeed all people everywhere, reason to remember that he had lived."

Abraham Lincoln

TIMELINE

1809

Abraham Lincoln is born February 12 in Hardin County, Kentucky

1834

Lincoln is elected to the Illinois General Assembly at age 25

1858

Lincoln and Stephen Douglas participate in a series of debates around the state of Illinois during their campaign for the U.S. Senate.

1862

Lincoln signs the Homestead Act into law May 20 and signs a law banning slavery in U.S. territories June 19

1863

Lincoln issues the Emancipation Proclamation January 1, symbolically freeing all slaves in the Confederacy

1842

Lincoln marries
Mary Todd

1846

Lincoln is elected
to the U.S. House
of Representatives

1861

Lincoln is inaugurated March 4;
southerners attack Fort Sumter,
in Charleston Harbor, on April 12,
initiating the American Civil War

1860

Lincoln is elected the 16th president of
the U.S.; South Carolina secedes from
the Union

1865

Lincoln is inaugurated a second
time March 4; General Robert E. Lee
surrenders to General Ulysses S. Grant
on April 9, ending the American Civil
War; Lincoln is shot April 14 and dies
April 15

1864

Lincoln is re-elected
president November 8

GLOSSARY

abolition—the immediate end of something, such as slavery

abolitionist—a person who works to end slavery

apprehension—worry or anxiety

asunder—broken into separate parts or pieces

casualties—people killed, wounded, or missing in a battle or in a war

despot—a ruler with total power who often uses it unfairly or cruelly

emancipation—the act of freeing someone from the control of another

incontestably—without a doubt

phenomenal—incredible

progressive—in favor of improvement, progress, and reform, especially in political or social matters

radical—in a political context, very socially progressive

secede—to withdraw from

transfigure—to transform

unorthodox—very unusual

unprecedented—exceptional or unparalleled

urbanized—characterized by dense populations and other qualities of city life

ADDITIONAL RESOURCES

FURTHER READING

Anderson, Michael. *Abraham Lincoln.* New York: Rosen Education, 2012.

Nardo, Don. *A Nation Divided: The Long Road to the Civil War.* Mankato, Minn.: Compass Point, 2010.

Press, David P. *Abraham Lincoln: The Great Emancipator.* New York: Crabtree, 2013.

INTERNET SITES

Use FactHound to find Internet sites related to this book. All of the sites on FactHound have been researched by our staff.

Here's all you do:

Visit *www.facthound.com*

Type in this code: 9780756549268

CRITICAL THINKING USING THE COMMON CORE

Abraham Lincoln's presidency changed the course of U.S. history, and the effects of these events are still felt today. Besides the Civil War and the end of slavery, which of Lincoln's actions do you think still has the most direct impact on you today? *(Integration of Knowledge and Ideas)*

Many historians have written about Lincoln's character and decision making. Which of his leadership qualities and personal qualities do you think made him most successful in steering the U.S. through crisis? *(Key Ideas and Details)*

Lincoln is famous for his speeches, which demonstrate his charisma and political genius. Choose a quote from one of Lincoln's speeches. What does the quote tell you about Lincoln's opinions and philosophies? What effect do you think the quote had on Lincoln's listeners in the North? In the South? What effect does the quote have on you? *(Craft and Structure)*

SOURCE NOTES

Page 6, line 4: "Cooper Union Address." Abraham Lincoln Online. 17 Feb. 2014. http://www.abrahamlincolnonline.org/lincoln/speeches/cooper.htm

Page 7, line 4: "Mr. Lincoln in New York." Lincoln Institute. 17 Feb. 2014. http://www.mrlincolnandnewyork.org/inside.asp?ID = 14&subjectID = 2

Page 9, line 6: Paul M. Angle, ed. *The Complete Lincoln-Douglas Debates of 1858.* Chicago: University of Chicago Press, 1990, p. 60.

Page 10, line 10: J. Matthew Gallman. *The Civil War Chronicle.* New York: Crown, 2000, p. 18.

Page 14, line 6: James M. McPherson. *Battle Cry of Freedom: The Civil War Era.* New York: Oxford University Press, 2003, p. 243.

Page 16, line 4: Michael Burlingame. *Abraham Lincoln: A Life.* Vol. 1. Baltimore, Md.: Johns Hopkins University Press, 2008, pp. 705–706.

Page 16, line 21: "First Inaugural Address." Abraham Lincoln Online. 17 Feb. 2014. http://www.abrahamlincolnonline.org/lincoln/speeches/1inaug.htm

Page 19, line 1: *Battle Cry of Freedom*, p. 249.

Page 21, line 6: T. Harry Williams. *Lincoln and His Generals.* New York: Vintage, 2011, p. iii.

Page 23, line 6: "Gettysburg Address." Abraham Lincoln Online. 17 Feb. 2014. http://www.abrahamlincolnonline.org/lincoln/speeches/gettysburg.htm

Page 25, line 17: "Second Inaugural Address." Library of Congress: American Memory. 17 Feb. 2014. http://memory.loc.gov/cgi-bin/query/r?ammem/mal:@field(DOCID + @lit(d4361300))#I486

Page 28, line 1: "Peoria Speech, October 16, 1854." National Park Service: Lincoln Home. 17 Feb. 2014. http://www.nps.gov/liho/historyculture/peoriaspeech.htm

Page 29, line 8: "House Divided Speech." Abraham Lincoln Online. 17 Feb. 2014. http://www.abrahamlincolnonline.org/lincoln/speeches/house.htm

Page 30, sidebar, line 7: "Fourth Debate: Charleston, Illinois." National Park Service: Lincoln Home. 17 Feb. 2014. http://www.nps.gov/liho/historyculture/debate4.htm

Page 31, line 6: Abraham Lincoln. "Letter to Horace Greeley, August 22, 1862." Abraham Lincoln Online. 17 Feb. 2014. http://www.abrahamlincolnonline.org/lincoln/speeches/greeley.htm

Page 32, line 7: "Emancipation Proclamation." National Archives and Records Administration: Featured Documents. 17 Feb. 2014. http://www.archives.gov/exhibits/featured_documents/emancipation_proclamation/transcript.html

Page 33, line 10: Francis B. Carpenter. *Six Months at the White House with Abraham Lincoln.* New York: Hurd and Houghton, 1866, pp. 269–270.

Page 35, line 2: Roy P. Basler, ed. *The Collected Works of Abraham Lincoln.* New Brunswick, N.J.: Rutgers University Press, 1953–1955, vol. 6, p. 410.

Page 40, line 5: Doris Kearns Goodwin. *Team of Rivals: The Political Genius of Abraham Lincoln.* New York: Simon and Schuster, 2005, pp. xvi–xvii.

Page 40, line 21: Douglas L. Wilson and Rodney O. Davis, eds. *Herndon's Informants: Letters, Interviews, and Statements about Abraham Lincoln.* Urbana: University of Illinois Press, 1998, p. 165.

Page 41, line 7: *Battle Cry of Freedom*, p. 450.

Page 42, line 19: "USDA Celebrates 150 Years." U.S. Department of Agriculture. 17 Feb. 2014. http://www.usda.gov/wps/portal/usda/usdahome?navid = USDA150

Page 45, line 7: *Battle Cry of Freedom*, p. 452.

Page 45, line 8: Leonard P. Curry. *Blueprint for Modern America: Nonmilitary Legislation of the First Civil War Congress.* Nashville: Vanderbilt University Press, 1968, p.1.

Page 50, caption: "Second Inaugural Address."

Page 51, line 7: Noah Brooks. *Washington in Lincoln's Time.* Whitefish, Mont.: Kessinger, 2007, p. 38.

Page 52, line 8: George S. Bryan. *The Great American Myth.* New York: Carrick and Evans, 1940, p. 189.

Page 54, sidebar, line 11: *Abraham Lincoln: A Life.* Vol. 2, p. 834.

Page 55, line 4: *Team of Rivals*, p. 747.

Page 56, line 6: Barack Obama. "Perfecting Our Union." *Atlantic*, 1 Dec. 2011. 17 Feb. 2014. http://www.theatlantic.com/magazine/archive/2012/02/perfecting-our-union/308832/

Page 56, line 11: James M. McPherson. *Abraham Lincoln.* New York: Oxford University Press, 2009, p. 65.

SELECT BIBLIOGRAPHY

Angle, Paul M., ed. *The Complete Lincoln-Douglas Debates of 1858.* Chicago: University of Chicago Press, 1990.

Basler, Roy P., ed. *The Collected Works of Abraham Lincoln.* New Brunswick, N.J.: Rutgers University Press, 1953–1955.

Bryan, George S. *The Great American Myth.* New York: Carrick and Evans, 1940.

Buell, Thomas B. *Combat Leadership in the Civil War.* New York: Crown, 1997.

Burlingame, Michael. *Abraham Lincoln: A Life.* Baltimore: Johns Hopkins University Press, 2008.

Catton, Bruce. *American Heritage New History of the Civil War.* New York: Viking, 2004.

Commager, Henry S., ed. *The Blue and the Gray: The Story of the Civil War as Told by Its Participants.* New York: Bobbs-Merrill, 1991.

Cuomo, Mario, and Harold Holzer. *Lincoln on Democracy.* Bronx, N.Y.: Fordham University Press, 2004.

Donald, David H. *Lincoln.* New York: Simon and Schuster, 1995.

Eicher, David J. *The Longest Night: A Military History of the Civil War.* New York: Simon and Schuster, 2001.

Gianapp, William E. *Abraham Lincoln and Civil War America.* New York: Oxford University Press, 2002.

Goodwin, Doris Kearns. *Team of Rivals: The Political Genius of Abraham Lincoln.* New York: Simon and Schuster, 2005.

Hyslop, Stephen G. *Eyewitness to the Civil War.* Washington, D.C.: National Geographic, 2006.

"Impact and Legacy of Abraham Lincoln." The Miller Center University of Virginia. http://millercenter.org/president/lincoln/essays/biography/9

McPherson, James M. *Abraham Lincoln.* New York: Oxford University Press, 2009.

McPherson, James M. *Battle Cry of Freedom: The Civil War Era.* New York: Oxford University Press, 2003.

Neely, Mark E., Jr. *The Last Best Hope of Earth: Abraham Lincoln and the Promise of America.* Cambridge, Mass.: Harvard University Press, 1993.

Oates, Stephen B. *The Whirlwind of War: Voices of the Storm, 1861–1865.* New York: HarperCollins, 1998.

Oates, Stephen B. *With Malice toward None: The Life of Abraham Lincoln.* New York: HarperCollins, 2011.

Randall, James G. *Lincoln the President.* New York: Da Capo, 1997.

Seidman, Rachel F., ed. *The Civil War: A History in Documents.* New York: Oxford University Press, 2001.

"Selected Speeches and Writings of Abraham Lincoln." Abraham Lincoln Online. http://www.abrahamlincolnonline.org/lincoln/speeches/speechintro.htm

INDEX

ABOUT THE AUTHOR

Historian and award-winning author Don Nardo
has written many books for young people about
history, including biographies of presidents Thomas
Jefferson and Franklin D. Roosevelt. Nardo lives
with his wife, Christine, in Massachusetts.